Shell Songs

Shell Songs

Poems by

James Miller

Kelsay Books

Cover by Chris Vellrath

ISBN: 978-1-947465-85-5

Kelsay Books
White Violet Press
www.kelsaybooks.com

In loving memory of my mother, Jane Blumgarten Miller

Acknowledgements

The Anglican Theological Review: "Buying a Map in Wisconsin"
Avocet: "Walking"
The Bella Online Literary Review: "While you're on the
   Respirator"
The Blue Unicorn: "Dawn," "Aging," "Vacation"
The Broadkill Review: "Reciting Waves," "With you on the
   Radio," "The Gardener," "Fire Escape"
The Dark Horse: "Walking Back from Work to Suburban Station"
Delaware Poetry Review: "Camping," "Pilgrimage," "Meeting
   Flora at the Resort"
Dream Catcher: "Dancing with Dana, A Factory Worker,"
   "Hometown Boys"
The Eclectic Muse: "Summer in Trenton," "Fog Dance"
The Gilbert W Perry Center for the Arts: "Shell Songs"
The Lyric: "Beach House," "Language," "To Mom on Mother's
   Day," and "For Lisa"
*No Place Like Here: an Anthology of Sussex County Poetry and
   Prose:* "Companion"
The Rockford Review: "The Ways She Looked"
The Rotary Dial: "Sunny Day," "Child on the Beach," "From
   Philbin Beach," "Martha's Vineyard," "Song of her Waiting,"
   "Grief's Work," "Measuring the Stars from Philbin Beach,"
   "After Laying your Ashes at Sea"
Simba: "She said"
Time of Singing: "Another Hospital Visit," "Standing at the
   Shore," "Talking a Friend into Rehab," "Reflections on Rehab
   in Florida.
Westward Quarterly: "Learning to Sing"

Contents

Child on the Beach

His steps are peaceful like the sea today
and in front of the next small, cresting wave
I watch him pick up shells to hear them say
this is the water your young mother gave
to you at birth; his tide-born eyes like birds
that have left sand to float on the ocean.
It will be years from now when those soft words
come back to him, come back when the motion
of schools and work have clogged his natural ears
and somewhere beyond that fog he will hear
his mother's voice on the far shore of songs
calling from island wombs where he belongs
and he'll know he must come back again to learn.
I know this child. I know he will return.

From Philbin Beach

Before leaving, I let your ashes go
for the same reason I welcome the wind
as walking I now part dunes powdered by snow
and leave a path on earth's fragile skin
where be it your ashes or the wind, tonight
this air that leads me back to sea
seems made of you as out of moonlight
that having no sky to hold it meets me
here, new, in white boots at the water.

Our Porch at Dusk

Again my breath becomes the sea
as we sit here to drink and rest,
to let the moon move in slowly
above the dunes as day digests.
I want to know your spirit's wave,
the one that calls you from the pack,
and rising inside your gaze
breaks to say you can now sail back
to me on our porch of dreams,
to us and to what love still means
now as the world drinks its blood
and thirsty still will start a flood
that we like most will not escape.
Still we will love before death's gate.

Martha's Vineyard

Here your voice calls back to me
as each next wave unrolls the sea
to my new life walking the shore,
hearing now what I heard before
when you said there's a castle to our love
that stands in sand as currents shove
the land to sea, the sea to land;
that you will always be the sand
and find me walking as if in a dream
in the hour of shells when winds seem
to carry your songs on each wave
and in that distance you will have no grave.

Returning to Battery Park

New Castle, DE

At first I thought your trees were tombs
and that your grass like a dried womb
had no room for me to return
or to be born again as from an urn.
But birds, again the summer birds
carry new songs as I do words,
and today years that blocked my way
seem to break towards a deeper day
when first I touched the childhood sand
that runs the river down your hand
and waits at your far walkway's end
with the dream I might start again
as when my mom told me her breeze
would find me here among the trees.

Evening Cast

At last the moon and fading ocean sky
like changing tides now move the day to stars,
to darker sands where my bright lures will fly
and fall alone into the current's arms.

By now the lovers have their sandy beers,
sunset runners pass with windy breath.
I like to cast until all I hear are waves,
and only night's long hymn is left.

Learning to Sing

Perhaps it was a bright feather
or the quick light of breaking clouds
when sudden wind pulled the weather
into a flashing sight of sound
where both the birds and sun became one
of many visions that must be sung.

Chartres at Night.

France, Summer 2016

I heard the bells and believed I could sing
when sunlight fell beneath the steeple's peak.
In darkness I then left as if with wings.

What clues inside the cathedral still ring
at midnight so I might not sleep but seek?
I heard the bells and believed I could sing.

For God was war—and faith his bloody king—
when in the moonlight bells said *let love speak.*
In darkness I then left as if with wings.

My voice, this growing string to which I cling,
now weaves through evening and will not be meek.
I heard the bells and believed I could sing.

And time, like death, which drips on everything,
is stopped tonight from its eternal leak.
In darkness I then left as if with wings.

For, yes, my shadow is what the light brings
and what I wear day by day, week to week.
I heard the bells and believed I could sing.
In darkness I then left as if with wings.

Sunny Day

And as the sand became a path I knew
from years before, and running children splashed
my past along the shore, I walked and grew
to who I was—the spreading smiles I passed
a tide that led me in the August sun.
And a new current called me out to swim
and let the waves tell me my day was done
as floating on my back I heard the hymn
of each wave washing off my wrinkled skin
to where with sea-born wings I would begin.

Aging

Even the falcon let go from its flight
and met the hard earth in my backyard woods.
I didn't meet it by day, but by night
when walking I knelt down and understood
with hands holding wings of moonlight
that the feathers I followed no longer fly;
my new directions are to say goodbye.

Plainbrook Cemetery

I like to think you're buried here
among the spring flowers at dawn—
and now with birds I hear
your soul from the brush as a fawn
leaps gravestones on its way
towards the lit fields with thoughts of day.
For everyday like a bell
I come to watch how death can bloom
above the soil's buried spell
with beds of roses, the breath of June.
And in the cemetery's glow
their names are yours, this grass your home.
A home locked in the wide green's eye
when suddenly birds start to fly.

Language

One dawn the sky set forth an ancient bird
with wings that pumping would become our words
as each day a feather fell from its flight
and landed on our tongues to then recite
the searching voyage from where we have grown,
the walking fields that have become our poems.

Standing at the Shore

As if the morning was my breath,
the first I'd taken since I left
two years before to find a home,
the ocean met me there alone
and let me hear inside the waves
her voice still echoing from the days
before we knew her death was near;
most likely months, at most a year.
I never thought her words would call
me out again, would come and fall
into me as the windy spray
wet my tight arms then blew away
and leaving only salt behind
allowed my tongue to lick and find
the taste my body once shared
with family, friends, the open air.
But more than that, she said *to leave,*
I am with you and you are free.

From a Dock at Night

After your death I left for sea.
I fled the grass where I had grown
because I could no longer be
a bird in fields where I had flown
or poems on a dawn-lit page
to ease my loss through words with age.
But tonight like a raft I drift
in the what if of counting stars—
what if the past could become mist?
What harbor would hold your arms?
For like a sailor's whose one vow
was to make it back somehow,
I hear your voice now from land
and pass through death from water to sand.

Measuring the Stars from Philbin Beach

Evening starts my sleepless smile
that stretches out all night to stars
I imagine are merely miles
like headlights from the sun-drawn cars
that will be parked here soon at dawn.

When morning joggers come, I leave,
and slowly walk back home with yawns
so deep I no longer believe
the sunlight wants me to wake up
or to go and walk to her grave
where my old flowers lay in lumps
with what the earth will let me save.

But still I smile the length of night,
the line that holds her life to mine
where in the darkness I take flight
from this hard earth as stars align
my memories to her light now,
and with the waves we walk somehow.

Vacation

Like the moon I push through each cloud
and like the lighthouse watch the sea
here on this porch and in the sound
of wind and waves, my soul set free
to believe I might belong here
one day at dawn just like the deer.

Beach House

Evening drops her purple hair
and weaves her locks through summer's glare
as from our porch, love, again
we stare and wait for stars like when
so young we walked this beach and blew
our breath's new songs beneath a moon
of white-lit foam, that salty spray,
our kiss the splash of breaking waves.
But now, if wet, our toes would numb
if we set out without the sun.
So each day we watch them,
the couples sailing at dusk; above
each one a map of distant skies
that shine for them just as the tides
we hope will carry them to shore
someday, to sandy steps and doors
that open with a breeze when years
like us tell them to stop and hear
this ebb and flow, the sea their breath;
this song that lives when we have left.

Another Hospital Visit

And, yes, the flowers are still there
tonight in our small garden where
they freshen the wind's breath with blooms.
At dawn, I searched for some to sooth
my shaking hands and bring to you.
These here spilled purple streams of dew
across my palms when I cut them.
And just as nature says amen
when buds unfold to meet the sky,
won't you please open your sweet eyes?

Grief's Walk

From nightmares with each eyelash
striking before dawn, I
walk away from each dream of ash
on a path I begin
by stepping out at dark
onto the dim-lit streets—birds
a blur of chirps across the park
as sliding through night's dew I turn
to meet the river. She'd sit here
as I do now on clear mornings
to watch the water and her years—
her smile a mask to death's warning,
bright hats on her bald head. She'd sit
here, waiting, knowing I'd visit.

To Mom on Mother's Day

In the undertow of your death
I leave the air to find your breath
in your new home beneath the sea
and wait for you to release me
in the bones of coral reefs
where I know a mermaid breathes
and waits for me like stretching sand
to bear a child again on land.
No longer will I search for more;
our child will walk the sandy shore.

The Baths of Lourdes

Not the ocean, but to the baths;
far from the waves where I was born
to now cup water in my hands

and drink until my breath
sings clean above each coming storm.
My prayers hatch in their floating nests.

After Laying your Ashes at Sea

Tonight the moon and all her stars
compose a song above the ocean, play waves
along the shore and back, back to the far
tides that moved them, out there where you wait.
Tonight I trust wind, its long hum
of futures, pasts, where to listen casts
a line out to where what's begun
remains a waking dream, a current too soft
for drowning, though in it you now sleep.

The Spy

I know with just a simple knock
she'd say *hello, come in, please sit*;
and for hours childhood would revisit
with jokes and stories to unlock.
But now I like to hide and wait
just as when I was a shy teen
for her to appear in bright scenes
on her back porch or at her gate.
There's still a secret song I keep
beneath the silence of my gaze
that waits for her until it plays
and carries me until I sleep.

For Lisa

In truth I thought I was the woods
and who I was was where I stood
in fading leaves—my lot a tree—
I never thought I'd find the sea
as today I walk its shore
and part small waves like open doors
that splash the past into a passing mist.
To think I've come so far upon your kiss.

Fog Dance

Inside the night there are too many stars
and if not stars there are too many dreams
to become hooked upon as if by moonbeams
that make me believe living with her is far
from this same earth that carries her ripe grave.
For I must still dance here, so let fog save
me these few hours to step out the door
into thick air where I see nothing more
than the new ghost that welcomes me.

Through eternity the trees have known this air
and loving their bright birds have offered nests
to birds that could not see from here to there—
I need to climb one now to find my breath.
Yes, this damp bark seems etched into my palm.
Now climb, James, climb. There still must be a song.

Each branch might break. Then again dancers fall,
and even as I shake the birds still call
to tell me there is something waiting here
for me to claim in this new atmosphere.

Like fragile leaves, my life seems made of sky
as I stretch farther into the tree's mind.
Wet hands don't slip. Not now before I find
my vision from the top. It's not that high.

Yes, here at last, the hanging view I need
of a dull day that only offers gray.
From here I plant my song, my dance, my seed.
I plant them here because death makes me pray
and though there is nothing left for me to see
if I fell I would die. This sets me free.

From Smith's Hill

Once again through the frosty mist
onto this hill where I once missed
my chance to say *I love you dear*;
those windy words now shout up here.
What are my constant snowy walks
but roads I follow as if I'm lost
and neither one can take me home?
I know them well but still I roam
and only find each day this hill,
this hell where I will shout until
you respond back to my lost pen;
please forgive me dear—let's try again.

Song of her Waiting

Sweet moon, let go your stars and lend my songs,
low as they are, a home to fill their holes
so they can play and calm the breath she longs
for me with, and the doubt that life just rolls
without a direction set out by you,
you the bright magician of what comes true.

Remembering my Mother

To remember your eyes
I gather shells,
and hold them to the sky
like painted bells
who lead by sight before sound
as sea-birds rise and then sweep down
to call the waves and wind,
the tides of shells I hear you in.

Night Lessons from Childhood

If the moon shaved to a slight hook
could catch my eyes and let me feel
poems I read by daylight's book,
I knew somehow my life is real,
a calling world that was my own,
each changing word becoming home.

First Kiss

By now you think I would be calm to lead
my lips to yours, and let my breath spread seeds
towards soft air we might share, secrets keep,
to finally seal my place beside you in sleep.
But we both move as slowly as we eat
and the time it takes for us to choose a meal
stands out in silence as if to repeat
how our burnt tongues have lost the taste to feel
what they still like or what they mean to say.
We both try hard not to look away
when the past arrives like an unwanted dish
the waiter insists we ordered. *But not this*
our shocked eyes respond, sliding from the table
like spilled ice to the floor, the bathroom door
becoming home as we're unable
to stop the tears that digest our lives.
And around us families smile—kids, husbands, wives.
But still we drive to shore after dinner
and walk the sand as if by moonlight's faith.
I hold your hand as stars align our place
to here and now; here as the breeze stirs
the salt of waves into a sailor's vow
where we again must trust the sea somehow.
For it's been years since I thought I could swim
against time's current towards love's island
to start a life born from another's touch.
I would have drowned then in the undertow's hush.
But tonight time with the sunset has left
and this new world of night seems made for us
who long for tides that flow to forget
the world that was, just let us love now.
Yes, now, as I dare make my little move.
Our bed at dawn begins here with the moon.

Reciting Waves

It's easier this way, driving off
until a road ends near the ocean.
That's because most roads keep moving
without you, as soon as your car stops,
and the door beside you quietly opens.
The dune grass that rubs your legs,
blowing as you walk its sandy stem,
is not like a road. The grass is soothing
because it sways in place, the sea's waves
repeating one sound up and down the shore.
Why we come back here again and again
is to forget the question of coming
or going. The rhythm we're looking for
began long ago. It is still humming.

With you on the Radio

Reception is breaking, your scratchy voice
half here, half there, clear for a soft second
before fading away. This car and radio
are what calm my hands now, my stubborn choice
to keep you on and listen, to still depend
on what I want to hear, what I want to hear.
But I didn't know where I would drive
searching for sound, for echoes
from a place and time when your songs were near.
What I've found are back roads, deep hills
spilling down valleys away from your sky.
If the next road takes me down far enough
to where, with static, your voice becomes still,
will you forgive silence—the peace I take back up?

The Gardener

The streets are awake to walk tonight,
a steam of summer breath—my voice, their voice,
voices taking off on curbs of yellow light
spreading from lit block to lit block this noise
that guards the city, noise that is safe.
Somehow I must thank these people
for keeping the moon, for securing space
under trees to pick blooms, sepals,
the scent of flower a sweet sweat inside my palms.
Sometimes I think I should hand them out
all night, my flowers, peddling until dawn,
saying, *friends, taste these, wet them with your mouth.*
But, oh, so often I just wait here, breathing,
a dark watchman of our gardens, quiet, dreaming.

Fire Escape

I walk because your window's open,
because your small room is like
a radio playing the city's songs.
And though you have no balcony, no chosen
bird to sing to tonight, I walk
waiting for your face—your chin to cheek
a slight rib of the moon sculpting grace.
And there's a rhythm you turn on
walking outside onto your scape to breathe.
I walk because breath still holds you,
your breath of breeze, sweat, faith; and when
your elbow rubs the railing, its point is smooth.
So smooth that the rub tickles you, you laugh.
I walk to stop where you stand. I stand to be moved.

Shell Songs

Is your whisper a wall
or a soft calling to my ear?
Like fog, you force me to walk slowly,
each step leading to sea.

      …

Voice splitting the mist of fog,
pounding waves on this gray beach,
you know I walk your shore invisible;
do you doubt I will sail?

I follow you because you leave no path,
no footprints in the dirt or sand.
I follow you because you trust the sea.
Storm after storm, you must know I know this.

...

Each day an island appears,
the people there with fruit and dance.
By dusk, they tell me they once saw you.
They know I cannot stay.

What lives in the breaking waves,
the spray of mist as I leave each island?
The mystery seems to rise from their shores,
spreading over their beaches, their homes.

     ...

Determined, I pulled anchor, set sail,
my hands could bend the wind. Now I
drift here, wingless on the sea's long breath.
I may never find you—only your direction.

Are you the bird in my dreams
or the wind that wakes me?
Each day these voices and visions
fade into one thing, the ocean.

...

Strange, as I am your follower
to imagine your escape. Sometimes I see
a shack, endless mist, but mostly I hear
the shells you placed to your ear.
I sing to remember this.

Windy grass, the spice of sand
blowing out to sea. Somehow these islands
seem closer to you now, as if you could
live on land that rests on water.

...

A seabird, feathers spread with wings
like sails—sometimes I think it's you, this bird
resting on my boat. Like you, it leaves
when it wants. I must remember it.

I did not wake for the bird
or in my sleep dream of it.
I did not scream for it to stay or leave.
I simply awoke at dawn—a feather beside me.

...

Near night I saw smoke,
saw your dark hair becoming sky.
An anchor, how you hid the moon
and stopped my tide, how for once
in my boat I waited, preparing for dawn.

The blinking light of water,
it saw as I touched your shore
dunes, bright with wind, dancing with birds
as I touched your shore.

      ...

You were picking berries—the basket full
at your feet. You took your time
then, the berries you had waited for, picking
and putting them in your mouth slowly,
each sweet bite.

Without words, we listened to your shells,
to winds that stir with the years
of your ocean. Calm, the air of the shell
you gave to me, my hand offering you
a feather.

     …

We sleep beneath spiders, crawling
spotted leaves, trees of heavy fruit
pushed by winds. Still you always sleep
and awake asking me only of my dreams.

What is this night dance, your arms outstretched
like a dark bird's wings? You tell me to leave the fire
and follow you through trees. You say no one
can see in the forest, so we sing. Sing.

. . .

Your skin, the thin fabric of your blood,
how at dusk it cools, easing you
into me. The fool you say came here,
his fists full of sand, feeling in it everything
but his skin.

Your feet seem to begin
where the sand and water meet,
the impressions you leave
filling in, moving on.

...

At every shore another wave,
another shell to land or sea.
It is this ebbing, where what returns
must leave; only the art of flowing
can replace such loss.

The Seagulls

Once when I was younger
descending from these dunes
onto this beach, I'm sure I found
them together, resting, sunning
their wings into
a washed sheet of light
by the water.
I can still see myself running
up to them, watching them break,
their wings cutting off
like small clouds
into a clear sky.

Companion

This is usually my small space
beneath the stars. Here, next to the river,
where my thoughts drift on an airy raft—
to the past, always to the past.

But tonight there's a dog here, a lab
or shepherd, this dog splashing in the water.
Licked with moonlight, it seems to shake off sleep,
dragging to shore all the branches and logs
the river offers.

Maybe it's because we've met by dark
and I haven't run away, it hasn't barked,
maybe this is why I believe the dog is mine?

But, no, it couldn't be mine, for it moves
too much like the river. As now, stepping
out of water onto sand, the dog stops to look back
at the current—the hum of ripples
that keeps it calm on land, still enough to sleep.

Somehow I believe this dog still sees itself
as part of the current. Of course, it must feel
its fur, wet on the beach, gathering flies.
But its senses, those pointed ears and staring eyes,
they seem to open to the river so easily—
as if tides only take us where we want to go.

Walking

There's a clause in me for you
that resists a finished line, an
ongoing breath in me for you
that exhales remembering
when we walked along this path.
Though what I remember now
is not our walking as much
as our walk's pause, that stretch
of untouched grass
where we would stop to rest,
where I would fall asleep
and waking find you there;
your face a shock of daylight,
flashes blinking into flesh.

Buying a Map in Wisconsin

I've yet to walk these cornstalks
or under a blue sky to stroll
one of these country roads.
Roads, which like blown seeds, skip
from field to field, and must lead somehow
to a house and story.
To me, these roads are only safe for driving,
a place where I look through my window to watch
oars of cornhusks rowing across a plain.

Though the more I drive, the more I know
someone like me does not come out so far
to get lost or let go. I have family here
in a small house in Patch Grove, Wisconsin.
And when I was a child, I remember burying
my grandmother there, where amidst the tears
of that morning, I marveled how butterflies
combed her tombstone with a spiritual air,
how my fingers changed states
tracing her name on a cut of marble rock.

Pilgrimage

Bells
angels my mom would say
walking into

each cathedral's cold breath.
It was strange to me, the stone floors,
my polished shoes and her heely

steps, the calling echo
as angels seemed so close,
awake and shining

through stained glass.
Today
revisiting each cathedral

I still hear that walking echo,
watching as the windows
seem to pull me

closer to the sun,
to the thought of angels
again. Mom never told me

when she prayed with nervous hands,
hands shaking back the sleeves
of her black dress,

how far I'd have to travel
to find my feet
on solid ground again—

she just put me in a pew
like this one, let me pray and stare.
She said it was good to see angels.

Hometown Boys

Driftwood from the river,
tides turning from water to shore,
tides that will today deliver
more and more
driftwood from the river.

At dusk they return from work
and gather wood on the beach together.
By dark they've dug their hearth.
Beside the fire, one remembers

how when he was in love
he used to carve her name
into different docks.
Beginning to talk, he says
how he saw Sara today,
though the *s* looked like *f*,
the last *a* now worn off.

She said

she would keep my poems
as long as they were hers.
No, not the words, she said,
or their lines. Instead,
she would keep my poems
as long as she could hear
my voice still missing.
My voice that does not
speak to her until
my day of writing ends.
As there and then
when we are finally
in our bed and drifting,
she is where she needs to be,
the only one still listening.

About your Temper

I prefer fading lanterns, sunsets
shading birds to the sea. I search
for what cools smoothly, like the cup of tea
I bring to you each morning, how its steam
drifts out, leaving your lips still slightly sweet.

Meeting Flora at the Resort

At night in bed
just a short walk from the ocean
I imagined her dreams
their winds
and where they had led her.
What tide was I?
What weather did I bring?
At dawn she would wake up
walk to the porch and stare.
With birds
 I listened to her sing.

Ars Poetica from Mercy Street

I stop here on Sundays to listen to her play.
Her songs are homeless, and the buildings
in which she plays change. Only the piano,
the return of chords carried by echoes,
lets me know from outside it's her.
I have not been in this building before.

The stairwell is old. Like a basement
it leads to a slanting light beneath the door.
The music does not become louder, only more clear
as I walk up the steps.

I believe she knows I was carried here by sound
and because of this allows me to enter—
the smooth length of her arms becoming sharp, exact
at the points of her fingers.

There is something to how her fingers push the keys
as if knowing one note from the absence of others
that makes me believe all songs echo to the silence of another.
She does not stop playing when I touch her shoulder.

The Ways She Looked

Usually, when she danced
across the streets too

drunk, it was the drivers
who were struck,

their cars stopped
by the red flash of hair,

caught by the glance
of her summer night's dress.

Like the matches
mouthing flames to her

cigarettes, she sparkled
until she lit

her candle for the night;
that man who now walks alone

stopping at the next street
to look left, right.

Walking Back from Work to Suburban Station, Philadelphia

I cared more about the cold,
the snow wrapping me in white
so even him, the homeless man
who reached for me
could not see me, my face
when I said *no, not now, no.*
You see there's Christ
and there's the cold
and in a blizzard
I don't pretend to walk with both.
Though it felt like heaven, Suburban Station,
its wet floor of boots and piss.
Warm again, I gave a dollar, I gave two,
and I guess to someone I was a saint—
No thank you.

hush

sweet honey, hush,
because the money
like tomorrow
is coming soon enough.
Don't you know
our skin will wrinkle
if our minds stay rushed.
I said the night's for loving—
come here, shaking hands,
come here.

Summer in Trenton

At midnight you're asleep
when outside a voice screams
then goes silent—then again the flashing sirens.
To call our room an island
is to forget our door, how the locks
shake whenever strangers knock
looking for dope or cash, pacing our floor
until they know they're lost and leave.
Still, to say as you sleep, that I want more
for us, one day a porch and breeze,
is to ask too much of time and place.
First I must understand your face,
your calm I call your unconscious rhyme;
where it can be so easy to sleep, as easy to die.

Dancing with Dana, a Factory Worker

First lady of the floor,
your cotton dress is torn. Still,
you put on the pulse of song
for dances that keep you warm.

To watch you now
broad and spent,
dancing off the workweek
with your sweat
washing your skin back

to the hour
your dance was born—
a child in the rain splashing
each puddle into spray.

On the Local Train

I stare at the length of her neck,
close my eyes, let go my breath—
I let my air taste her sweat,
that heat beneath her hair, salt
of a workday done.

Talking a Friend into Rehab

The ocean will not freeze tonight
and moonlight makes the snow now as bright
as the old stars we know gave birth to it.
Leave with me now. It's cold, but the spit
you kiss into the wind will freeze into a song.
Trust me, you'll be back. It won't be that long.

Reflections on Rehab in Florida

And when the final seizure left my mouth,
my foamy lips became the stranded beach
of sinking breath that might still rise to reach
a land away from northern storms, far south
where sunlight waited for me not to drink.
Having now returned home, I often think
about the day I met sweet, sober air.
I call it a sense the once shaking share
where sitting still is enough to spark a smile
and waiting an hour in line is no long mile
because the day is worth the food you eat
and by the grace of God you still have feet.

The Sailor

The world turns around me
slowly, quickly,
shifting with the tides—
I sail alone seeking shelter
on a sea of verse and rhyme.
Take me to bed,
hold me as we lie;
I need the comfort of a friend,
the warmth of your thigh.

An Ocean's Son

Just stare at her
The moon sheen of wonder,
And forget about your life
Forget about your hunger
As you just stare at her
The moon sheen of wonder.
Yes, hold onto her
Like a dying lover's breath,
For she that is we
Is in you what is best.
Yes, just stare at her
The moon sheen of wonder
And be happy to be
Of her and of under.

About the Author

James Miller began writing poetry as a student in the English department at the University of Wisconsin, Madison. After receiving his Bachelor of Arts in creative writing, James continued to New York University where he completed his Master of Fine Arts in poetry. Today he lives and writes in New Castle, Delaware, where he won the state award for an emerging poet through the Delaware Division of the Arts. James attends and reads at various literary events throughout the state and his poems have been published widely both in the USA and abroad. James Miller is also a songwriter and his songs can be heard on YouTube using the user name JamesMiller82. You can also contact him on his email at jom232@gmail.com. As with all things, he owes much thanks to his friends and family, particularly his brother and father, for their kindness and support.